31 DAYS OF POSITIVE SELF-TALK

By

Danario Lankford

All rights reserved.
No part of this book may be reproduced, stored in a retrieval system, or transmitted in any form without written permission from the author, except by reviewers who may quote brief excerpts in connection with a review. For information regarding this please write to: Danario Lankford at danario.lank@gmail.com.

Table of Contents

What Is Positive Self-Talk? 5
Introduction 6
Day 1: I Am Love 7
Day 2: I Am Great 9
Day 3: I Am Strong 11
Day 4: I Am Healthy 13
Day 5: I Am Confident 15
Day 6: I Am Humble 17
Day 7: Go Live 19
Day 8: Be The Change 21
Day 9: I Will Win 23
Day 10: I Am Grateful 25
Day 11: I Am Motivation 27
Day 12: Success Is Mine 29
Day 13: Do Not Give UP 31
Day 14: I Am Free 33

Day 15: I Am Purpose 35
Day 16: I Am Happy 37
Day 17: I Am Resilient.. 39
Day 18: I Will Preserve 41
Day 19: Learn To Be Patient 43
Day 20: I Am Consistent 45
Day 21: More Than Enough 47
Day 22: Think Big... 49
Day 23: A New Day 51
Day 24: I Have Hope... 53
Day25: I Pray 55
Day 26: Keep Your Head Up.................................. 57
Day 27: Think Positive.. 59
Day 28: I Am 61
Day 29: I Am Kind 63
Day 30: Champions Finish Strong 65
Day 31: God Has A Plan.. 67
Author Note.. 69

What Is Positive Self-Talk?

Positive self-talk is the practice of talking to oneself in a kind, compassionate, and encouraging manner.

It is about creating a positive inner dialogue that builds you up, increases motivation, and makes you feel good about yourself and your abilities.

So instead of telling yourself "I can't do it" or "This is impossible", you can choose to say "I can do this" or "All things are possible with God."

Negative self-talk tends to focus on preconceived ideas that we are not good enough, always a failure, or cannot do anything right, but that is not true, because you are good enough.

You can do anything you put your mind to.

Introduction

What can 31 Days Of Positive Self Talk do for you?

31 Days Of Positive Self Talk will help you **boost your inner confidence** and **belief within self** because when life gets hard, it is natural to focus on the negative aspects.

This book will empower you to focus on the positive in life and not just that but give you a whole new outlook of how you see yourself and others.

So, for the next 31 Days take this book with you wherever you go and always affirm yourself throughout your day to keep that positive energy flowing.

DAY 1

I Am Love

I am love I love me and others. I am created to love because God is love and love is power. Love holds no wrong because love is gentle and strong.

> "Love holds no wrong because love is gentle and strong."

DAY 2

I Am Great

I am great when I look in the mirror, I see greatness because greater is he that is inside of me than he that is in the world. Now go be great.

> "Greater is he that is inside of me than he that is in the world."
> *[1 John 4:4]*

DAY 3

I Am Strong

When I feel weak, I feel strong because the Lord keeps me strong. I will keep climbing, I will keep pressing, I will keep holding on. This is just a reminder that I am strong.

> *"This is just a reminder that I am strong."*

DAY 4

I Am Healthy

I am healthy.

My mind is healthy.

My body is healthy.

My life is healthy.

When I exercise, I feel healthy so that means I am healthy.

> "My mind is healthy my body is healthy my life is healthy."

DAY 5

I Am Confident

I am confident I am bold to go live my life achieving my dreams and goals. I am confident I am strong to keep winning beyond what is going on.

> *"I am confident I am bold to go live my life achieving my dreams and goals."*

DAY 6

I Am Humble

I am humble I am meek because I know it is not just about me, I am humble I am meek for what the future holds and all the joy it is going to bring.

> "I am humble I am meek because I know it is not just about me."

DAY 7

Go Live

I am living my life to the fullest, removing all barriers of worry, doubt, and fear. I am living my life to the fullest putting all negativity in the rear. Now I walk by faith because I must go live.

> "Now I walk by faith because I must go live."

DAY 8

Be The Change

Change starts from within yes change is perfect. Change is not bad because your life deserves it. Change is patient, yes change takes time, but all change is worth it.

> "Change is patient, yes change takes time, but all change is worth it."

DAY 9

I Will Win

If you quit, then how will you see your wins do not count yourself out but count yourself in. Now affirm to yourself every day I will win, I will win, yes; I will win.

> "I will win I will win yes; I will win."

DAY 10

I Am Grateful

I am grateful for my friends and family. I am grateful that grace has found me. I am grateful for the air that I breathe. I am grateful for the green grass, clean water, and beautiful trees.

> "I am grateful for my friends and family."

DAY 11

I Am Motivation

Look in the mirror and smile because you are worth it. You come a long way yes, every wonderful thing you deserve it. Many times, your thoughts said quit but you did not give in because your motivation said go win.

> *"Many times, your thoughts said quit but you did not give in because your motivation said go win."*

DAY 12

Success Is Mine

Success is mine, no success is not a crime, the path gets tough at times, but I must work hard for mine. So put success next to my name because I worked hard to get here, and it was not a game.

> "Success is mine no success is not a crime."

DAY 13

Do Not Give UP

Do not give up, go try it again because quitting is not an option but winning is.

Do not give up, go try it again because this time you may win.

Do not give up, go try it again.

> *"Do not give up, go try it again because quitting is not an option but winning is."*

DAY 14

I Am Free

I am free, my mind is free. I am free to be me. I am free to have freedom of speech. I am free so please take the labels off me. I repeat I am free I am free I am free.

> "I repeat I am free I am free I am free."

DAY 15

I Am Purpose

I have goals and a plan to achieve. I am purpose I know I have enormous potential inside of me. Now go aim high and be the best that you can be.

> *"I have goals and a plan to achieve. I am purpose I know I have enormous potential inside of me."*

DAY 16

I Am Happy

I am happy today is a wonderful day.

I am happy my life is fulfilled with grace.

I always smile because I am happy every day.

> "I always smile because I am happy every day."

DAY 17

I Am Resilient

I know life can get tough and difficult at times no lie I fell a few times, but giving up is not something that I will try because I am resilient.

> "Giving up is not something that I will try because I am resilient."

DAY 18

I Will Preserve

Through all the storms I had to preserve because if I did not preserve, I would not be here. Now as I affirm myself when I look in the mirror, I will always tell myself I will preserve.

> *"I will always tell myself
> I will preserve."*

DAY 19

Learn To Be Patient

It is not just about waiting but, in the waiting, what are you doing while you are being patient. No more complaining but work in silence and understand why it is important to be patient. Being patient can build and being patient is the key that can help all things heal.

> "Being patient can build and being patient is the key that can help all things heal."

DAY 20

I Am Consistent

Consistency is the key to unlocking the door to your dream. I have faith o yes; I believe that if I remain consistent, I can accomplish anything.

> *"I have faith o yes; I believe that if I remain consistent, I can accomplish anything."*

DAY 21

More Than Enough

You are more than enough, yes you can do phenomenal things.

You are more than enough look at the value you bring.

You are more than enough so stay strong and continue to say positive things.

"You are more than enough yes you can do phenomenal things."

DAY 22

Think Big

Think big, you were not created to think small.

Think big and believe that your life can evolve.

Think big because there is no more room to think small.

> *"Think big and believe that your life can evolve."*

DAY 23

A New Day

It is a new day for a renewed mind and a clean heart.

It is a new day for a fresh start.

It is a new day for a walk in the park.

It is a new day to let your creativity spark.

> "It is a new day for a renewed mind and a clean heart."

DAY 24

I Have Hope

Hope is bold to have hope is strong. Having hope will strengthen you to keep pressing on. Hope is not a lie because hope is alive and having hope is the reason that I shall thrive.

> *"Hope is bold to have hope is strong. Having hope will strengthen you to keep pressing on."*

DAY 25

I Pray

I pray for love, joy, hope, and peace. I pray that I am a better me. I pray that this will be a better day. I pray that God will make a way. I pray for this every day.

> *"I pray that this will be a better day.
> I pray that God will make a way."*

DAY 26

Keep Your Head Up

[2 Timothy 4:5]

Keep your head up no matter what happens. Do not give up when times are hard. Work to spread the good news and do everything God has given you to do.

> *"Do not give up when times are hard."*

DAY 27

Think Positive

Think positive and do the best you can.

Think positive, do not let the negative in.

Think positive because now you are a positive man.

> *"Think positive because now you are a positive man."*

DAY 28

I Am

I am more than a conqueror. I am living the life of my dream. I have faith I believe I can do remarkable things. I am love; I am joy I am peace. I am successful, I believe in me. I am powerful, I am confident I am unique.

> "I am more than a conqueror. I am living the life of my dream. I have faith I believe I can do remarkable things."

DAY 29

I Am Kind

I am kind, it is like love, it does not cost a thing. I am kind because one kind gesture can change a lot of things. I am kind just watch how many smiles it brings.

> *"I am kind it is like love it does not cost a thing."*

DAY 30

Champions Finish Strong

Look at how far you have come at times you wanted to quit but you did not give up. The race was long, but you prolonged because champions finish strong.

> "The race was long, but you prolonged because champions finish strong."

DAY 31

God Has A Plan

For I know the plans I have for you, declares the Lord, plans to prosper you and not to harm you, plans to give you hope and a future.

> *"For I know the plans I have for you," declares the Lord, "plans to prosper you and not to harm you."*
> ***[Jeremiah 29:11]***

Author Note

You finished this book congratulations champion remember champions finish strong.

Well, I hope this book empowered you to be a more positive, stronger, and better person in your day-to-day life.

Take it one day at a time and read a page a day to keep the positive momentum going.

God bless you and I wish you the best.

Sincerely, Danario.

To stay in touch with Danario you can email him at danario.lank@gmail.com

Made in the USA
Middletown, DE
27 November 2024